KWAME
Alexander

by Abby Cooper

CAPSTONE PRESS
a capstone imprint

Bright Idea Books are published by Capstone Press
1710 Roe Crest Drive, North Mankato, Minnesota 56003
www.mycapstone.com

Library of Congress Cataloging-in-Publication Data
Library of Congress Cataloging-in-Publication Date is available on the Library of Congress
website.
ISBN: 978-1-5435-5792-3 (library hardcover)
978-1-5435-6037-4 (paperback)
978-1-5435-5824-1 (eBook PDF)

Editorial Credits
Editor: Claire Vanden Branden
Designer: Becky Daum
Production Specialist: Colleen McLaren

Quote Source
p. 4, "Newbery Medal Acceptance Speech." *ALSC*, 2015

Photo Credits
Alamy: ZUMA Press, Inc./Alamy, 16; AP Images: Andrew Wardlow/The News Herald, 19, Matt
Sayles, cover; Getty Images: Katherine Frey/The Washington Post, 25; Newscom: Birdie Thompson/
AdMedia, 5, 28, Johnny Louis/JL/Sipa USA, 23; Rex Features: Matt Sayles/AP, 26; Shutterstock
Images: Anna Sheppard, 6–7, 8, 14–15, Anutr Yossundara, 30–31, atm2003, 20–21, Maks Ershov,
11; Yearbook Library: Yearbook Library, 13

TABLE OF CONTENTS

CHAPTER 1

BEING Kwame

"Write a poem that is **contagious**. Let it **inspire**," Kwame Alexander said. He had ended his speech. The crowd clapped. He had just won the Newbery Medal. He won it for his book *The Crossover*. Alexander was happy. The book had taken five years to write. He had worked very hard.

Kwame Alexander enjoys writing for kids of all ages.

THE JOHN NEWBERY MEDAL

The John Newbery Medal is an award given out each year. It is for the best American books for children.

The Crossover is told through poetry. It is about twin brothers who play basketball. They are 12 years old. Alexander wrote about what had mattered to him at that age. He wrote about sports, family, and friends.

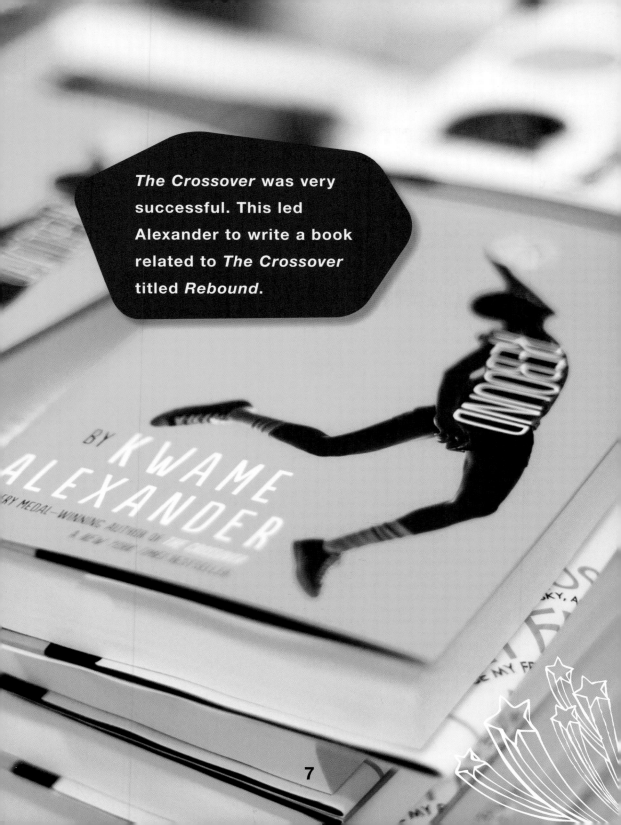

The Crossover was very successful. This led Alexander to write a book related to *The Crossover* titled *Rebound*.

7

Alexander attended a book fair with award-winning author James Patterson (right) in 2018.

Kids of all ages read *The Crossover*. They love it. Adults do, too. The book has won many awards.

CHAPTER 2

AWARD-WINNING Writer

Alexander was born on August 21, 1950. He was born in New York. He grew up around books. His father **published** them. His mother taught English.

Alexander grew up in Manhattan, New York.

Alexander started writing when he was 12. He wrote a Mother's Day poem. It made his mother happy. He learned more about poetry in college. Later, he wrote poems for his wife. Alexander kept writing. He has not stopped since.

FIRST NAME

Kwame is Alexander's middle name. His first name is Edward.

Alexander was a member of the newspaper staff in junior high.

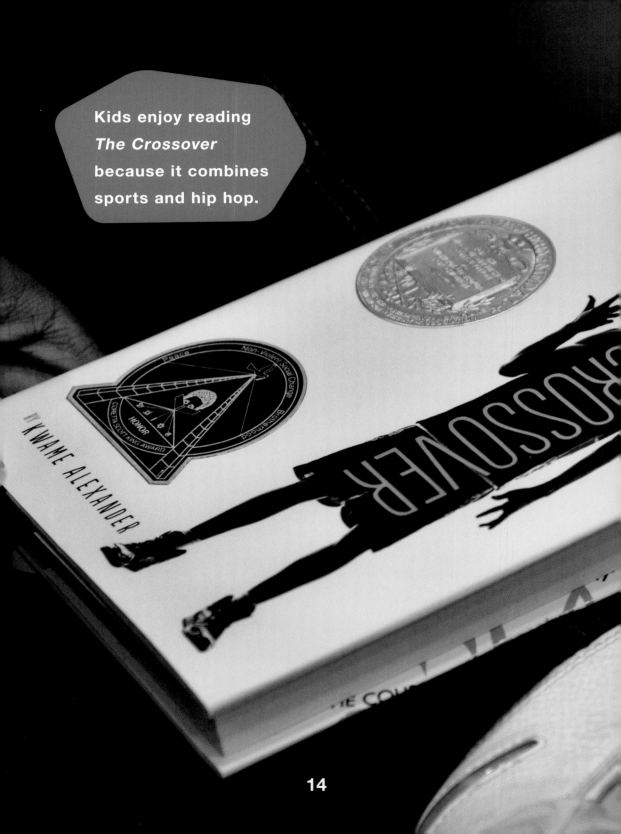

Kids enjoy reading *The Crossover* because it combines sports and hip hop.

BIG SUCCESS

Alexander has written more than 20 books. He writes for children and adults. He is best known for *The Crossover*. It came out in 2014.

But Alexander's road to success was not easy. Publishers turned down *The Crossover* more than 20 times. They didn't think kids wanted a book about poetry and sports. They were wrong. Finally a publisher agreed to print the book. It became a big success.

Alexander's book *Solo* was published in 2017.

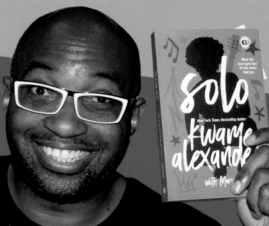

Alexander wrote more books about poetry and sports. His books are also about family, friendship, and love. His list of books continues to grow.

BEST SELLERS

Alexander has written six best-selling books.

CHAPTER 3

LENDING a Hand

Alexander likes to help others. So he started Book-in-a-Day in 2006. The program taught students about writing and publishing. Students left with a strong piece of writing. Book-in-a-Day ran for nine years.

Alexander still helps kids. He does this in many ways. He visits schools and libraries. He travels the country. He meets as many kids as he can. He has a positive impact on everyone he meets.

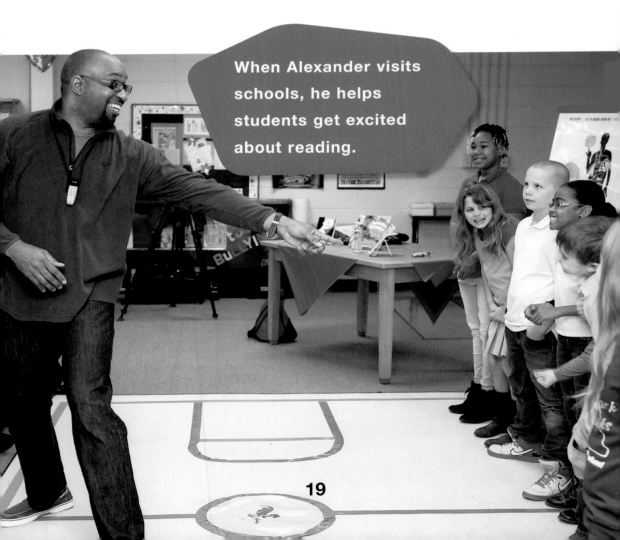

When Alexander visits schools, he helps students get excited about reading.

LEAP for Ghana
helps children in
Ghana, Africa.

LEAP FOR GHANA

In 2012, Alexander created LEAP for Ghana. He did this with writer Tracy Chiles McGhee. LEAP for Ghana helps African kids and adults. The program brings books and schooling to people who need them. On its first trip, the group built a library. Alexander continues to travel to Ghana. He makes a difference in communities near and far.

HEALTH CARE

LEAP for Ghana also brings health services to people who need them.

CHAPTER 4

LOOKING
Ahead

Alexander leads a busy life. He writes, speaks, and travels. He spends time with his wife and daughters. He comes up with new projects.

Alexander attends many book fairs where he talks to audiences about writing.

In 2017, Alexander started an online show called *Bookish*. He talks to other writers on the show. He also continues to write new books. His book *Rebound* was published in 2018.

Alexander also makes music based on his books. He works with his friend Randy Preston. They have even made music videos.

Alexander loves talking to kids about his books.

Alexander wants to publish books from people whose voices have never been heard.

26

A BIG IDEA

Alexander wanted more people to tell stories. In 2018, he created an **imprint** called Versify. Many of the books are also written with poetry. Alexander wants to publish books that touch kids.

GLOSSARY

contagious
spread from one person
to another

imprint
a brand name under which
books are published

inspire
fill someone with the urge
to do something or feel
something creative

publish
to prepare and issue a book
for public sale

TIMELINE

1950: Kwame Alexander is born on August 21 in New York City, New York.

1993: Alexander's first book is published.

2012: Alexander starts LEAP for Ghana.

2015: Alexander's book *The Crossover* wins the John Newbery Medal.

2018: Alexander starts his own imprint, Versify, at Houghton Mifflin Harcourt Books for Young Readers.

ACTIVITY

Poetry is very important in Alexander's books and in his life. Now, it's your turn to give poetry a try. Create your own poems using some of the same styles Alexander uses in his books.

To write an acrostic poem, pick a word, such as your name or favorite animal. Write the word vertically. Then, next to each letter, write another word that begins with the letter and describes your first word.

A list poem can be a list of people, places, items, or ideas. List poems are often funny when writers include things that are unexpected or unusual.

Free verse poems do not follow any rules. They can be whatever the writer wants. Choose a topic, put your pencil on the paper, and let the words flow!

31

FURTHER RESOURCES

Want to get to know Alexander even better? Enjoy these interviews:

Kwame's Frequently Asked Questions
http://kwamealexander.com/about/me/c/199

Reading Rockets
http://www.readingrockets.org/books/interviews/alexander/transcript

Sports Illustrated Kids
https://www.sikids.com/si-kids/2016/01/12/author-interview-kwame-alexander

Ready to learn more about Alexander's other projects? Check this out:

LEAP for Ghana
http://www.leapglobal.org/

McGrath, Brian S. *Game Changers: Kwame Alexander.* Huntington Beach, CA: Teacher Created Materials, 2017.

INDEX